Origami
Paper Animals

Didier Boursin

FIREFLY BOOKS

A FIREFLY BOOK

Published by Firefly Books Ltd. 2001

Copyright © Dessain & Tolra/HER 2000
Original title: Animaux de papier. Larousse.

Fourth printing 2008

U.S. Cataloging-in-Publication Data
   (Library of Congress Standards)

Boursin, Didier.
    Origami animals / Didier Boursin. – 1st ed.
[64] p.: col. ill.; cm.
Summary: 28 different origami designs of wild animals and pets.
ISBN-13: 978-1-55209-628-4 (bound)
ISBN-10: 1-55209-628-9 (bound)
ISBN-13: 978-1-55209-622-2 (pbk.)
ISBN-10: 1-55209-622-X (pbk.)
1. Origami. 2. Animals in art. 3. Paper work. I. Title.
736.982   21   2001

Published in the United States by
Firefly Books (U.S.) Inc.
P.O. Box 1338, Ellicott Station
Buffalo, New York, 14205

National Library of Canada Cataloguing Publication Data

Boursin, Didier
    Origami animals
ISBN-13: 978-1-55209-628-4 (bound)
ISBN-10: 1-55209-628-9 (bound)
ISBN-13: 978-1-55209-622-2 (pbk.)
ISBN-10: 1-55209-622-X (pbk.)

1. Origami—Juvenile literature. 2. Animals in art—Juvenile literature.
I. Title.
TT870.B683 2001   j736'.982   C2001-93071-5

Published in Canada by
Firefly Books Ltd.
66 Leek Crescent
Richmond Hill, Ontario L4B 1H1

Photography: Cactus Studio—Fabrice Besse
Cover interior design and layout: Nicolas Piroux
Editor: Mélanie Bauer-Giordana
Editorial Director: Catherine Franck-Dandres
Technical Co-ordination: Jacques Deffarges
Photoengraving: Nord Compo
Translation and Origami consultation: John Reid

Printed in China

Acknowledgments

I wish to thank all those who, from near or far, helped me to create this book. I thank the talented marbler Vincent Rougié for his elaborately wrought and multi-colored papers. I thank my children, Nina and Angelo, who participated with enthusiasm at all stages of the book. I thank Fabrice Besse, who has patiently photographed my paper folds for many years. I thank the editorial team and particularly Melanie. I thank equally those who appreciate my work and invite me to show my paper folds. I am grateful for Setsuko's advice and good nature.

You may send your comments and personal experiences to me at:
Didier Boursin
Boutique Setsuko et Didier
17, rue Sainte-Croix-de-la-Bretonnerie, 75004 Paris

Instructions		4
	Levels of Difficulty	4
	Symbols	4
	Bases	4
	Diagrams	4
	Principal Folds	5
	Details of the Bases	5
	Papers	7
	Sizes	7
	Folding and Cutting	7
▶	Fish	8
▶	Owl	10
▶	Elephant	12
▶▶▶	Heron	14
▶▶	Penguin	16
▶▶	Dove	18
▶▶▶	Bird	20
▶▶▶	Hen...	22
▶	... and the Chick	24
▶▶	Panther	26
▶▶▶	Eagle	28
▶	Whale	30
▶▶▶	Cat	32
▶▶	Horse	34
▶▶	Dog	36
▶▶▶	Crab	38
▶▶	Giraffe	40
▶▶	Rabbit	42
▶▶	Dragonfly	44
▶▶▶	Frog	46
▶▶	Sheep	48
▶▶	Parrot	50
▶	Seal	52
▶▶	Grasshopper	54
▶▶	Mouse	56
▶▶▶	Bull	58
▶	Turtle	60
▶▶▶	Monkey	62

▶ Beginner
▶▶ Intermediate
▶▶▶ Advanced

Instructions

"So, inanimate objects, do you have a soul?"

Poetic Meditations

Alphonse de Lamartine

For this book I have created 28 animals to which I have given an expression, a movement, sometimes a look, and almost a soul. Every fold is a humorous wink at life. The models are worked out meticulously, down to the smallest details, while adhering to the spirit of creating a work of art in paper, with the minimum of folds required to achieve a beautiful effect.

Have you ever seen a heron spreading out his wings before flight, a panther lazing in the sun, a mouse sniffing a good piece of cheese? It is up to you to continue these stories by imagining what follows. Paper is a material as noble as wood and stone. This book is the expression of a modern designer who sculpts paper in an ephemeral way as others capture the moment by a photograph or a poem.

Folding paper is also a thought game, a logical development where someone's nimble fingers fold a simple sheet of paper to result in an absolutely personal portrayal of an animal, with the hope that it is sufficiently expressive to be recognized by others.

I wanted to dress my animals in fur or feathers by using beautiful papers in dazzling colors without ever wanting to reproduce reality. I hope that these poetic folds will make people think about our environment and our planet where certain species are disappearing one by one. I hope that you will derive as much pleasure as I do in producing these magnificent animals, some of which are truly small masterpieces.

Levels of Difficulty

In the summaries, the paper-foldings are marked according to three levels of difficulty:
beginner ◗, intermediate ◗◗, and advanced ◗◗◗.
You should start with the easiest ones. To succeed in making a fold, you need time, a sense of calm, and patience. Some people will not succeed in making the animal in their first attempt. Don't let this discourage you; the second try is often better than the first. If you stumble over a step, let your work sit for a few hours, or even several days. This will often allow you to approach the paper-folding with a new spirit and will get things moving again.

Symbols

Before beginning, you should practice with ordinary paper to make the mountain fold and valley fold, as well as the reverse folds that are used in all the models.

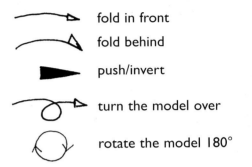

fold in front

fold behind

push/invert

turn the model over

rotate the model 180°

Bases

By combining some of the folds, you will achieve the bases needed to begin several animals in this book. In time, your fingertips will fold them automatically without your needing to look at the diagrams. With the preliminary base, you make the horse. With the bird base, you make the heron, the bird, the parrot and the dragonfly. With the fish base, you make the fish, the chicken, the elephant and the panther. With the water-bomb base, you make the seal and the eagle. The frog base is used for the frog and the crab. The other animals don't use any of these bases.

Diagrams

Every fold is explained step by step by the outline drawings. To achieve the folds, study the drawing carefully as well as the explanatory text instructions. Sometimes the diagrams are broken down into smaller details for head, feet, and so on. You should complete all these details before going on to the next step. The parts in color indicate that they are the reverse of the sheet of paper.

Principal folds

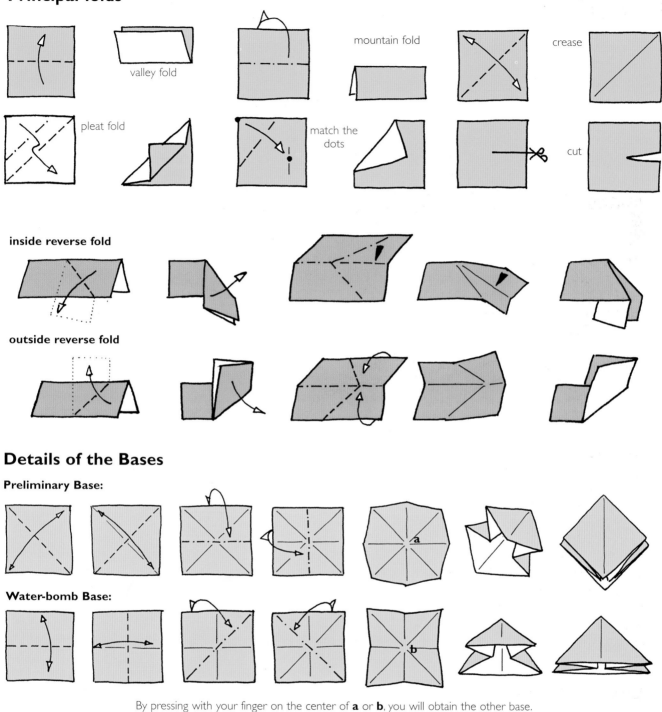

valley fold

mountain fold

crease

pleat fold

match the dots

cut

inside reverse fold

outside reverse fold

Details of the Bases

Preliminary Base:

a

Water-bomb Base:

b

By pressing with your finger on the center of **a** or **b**, you will obtain the other base.

Bird Base:

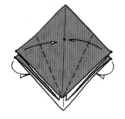

1. Make a preliminary base, then fold the bottom edges to the central fold.

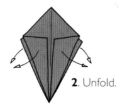

2. Unfold.

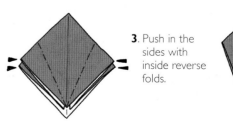

3. Push in the sides with inside reverse folds.

Fish Base:

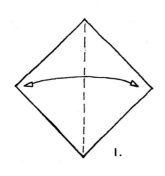

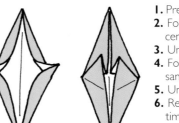

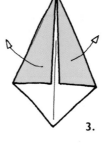

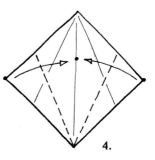

1.   2.   3.   4.

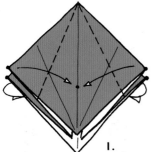

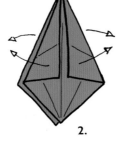

5.   6.   7.

1. Precrease as shown, vertically.
2. Fold the upper edges toward the central fold.
3. Unfold.
4. Fold the bottom edges in the same way.
5. Unfold.
6. Refold the edges at the same time as you pinch the side points.
7. Lay the base flat, placing the points up.

Frog Base:

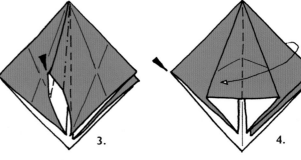

1.   2.   3.   4.

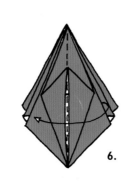

5.   6.

1. Fold the upper edges on both sides of a preliminary base.
2. Unfold.
3. Lift up a vertical flap, then open it by flattening.
4. Repeat the same fold with the other three flaps.
5. Lift up a layer while folding the points in half.
6. Turn a flap and repeat this fold with the other three sides.

Horse Base:

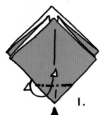

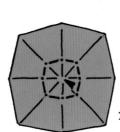

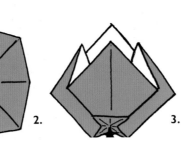

1.   2.   3.

1. To make this base for the horse's belly, fold all the layers front and back, then unfold completely.
2. Mountain fold the central square, then push in its middle to sink the square.
3. In the center of the square, the diagonals are valley folds and the medians are mountain folds. Lay the base flat as in the beginning.

Papers

The best papers are those that crease well and are sufficiently strong for repeated folding and unfolding, with a weight between 70 and 90 grams (20 to 24 lb. bond weight). Avoid papers that tear after several folds, such as certain recycled papers. White or colored papers that are used for photocopying or computer printing, as well as drawing papers that are not too thick, are excellent for folding. In stores that specialize in art and craft supplies, you will find a variety of marbled and decorated papers. And in everyday or unexpected places you will also find

many other fancy papers that will represent an animal with just the effect that you want. For example, the parrot was made from a recycled advertising flyer.

Sizes

Essentially, you will use squares and half-squares. Certain simple folds can be made in small sizes of paper; others, such as the heron, have numerous layers and require a larger size and a thinner paper. For experienced folders, any size of square will work. As a rule of thumb, it's best to start big, and then work down to smaller squares as you gain expertise.

You may purchase square Origami paper or cut your own squares from a sheet of letter-sized or A4 paper. (Origami instructions often refer to A4 paper. To get the proportion of an A4 sheet, trim ⅛ inch from the width of a letter-sized sheet.)

Folding and Cutting

A folding bone in wood or plastic is used in certain situations to make a crease by applying the flat side of the tool to achieve the fold.

Scissors are used to multiply the number of feet (the crab), to create the whiskers (panther), ears (rabbit), and crest (heron).

Birds' Legs:

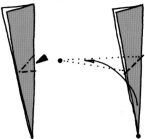

3. Refold toward the right.

4. Unfold completely.

6. Fold in half while placing the triangle's sides into a mountain fold.

I. The fold is made in two steps.

2. Fold up the point to the horizontal.

5. Mountain fold the two upper sides of the triangle, then valley fold the last point of the triangle.

Foot/Beak:

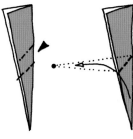

3. Fold the point down. To make a beak, fold the point toward the right to lie parallel.

4. Unfold completely.

 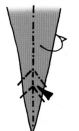  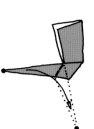 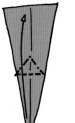

I. To achieve this fold.

2. Fold up the point to the horizontal.

5. Mountain fold and valley fold as indicated, then fold twice toward the vertical fold.

6. Fold flat.

Fish

▶ Beginner

The fish rest on three supporting points, giving the illusion that they are swimming in the water, drifting along with the current. It's up to you to create a lively school of fish in movement.

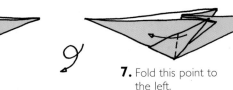

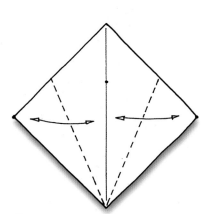

1. After creasing the diagonal of a square, fold and unfold the lower edge to the center crease.

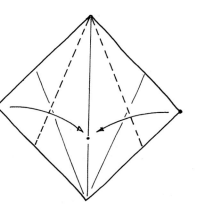

2. Fold the upper edges in the same way.

3. Fold the corners up using the creases from Step 1 and the new mountain fold indicated.

4. Cut along the bold line and fold the model in two to the rear.

5. Fold one point down vertically.

6. Mountain fold this point to the other side. Turn over.

7. Fold this point to the left.

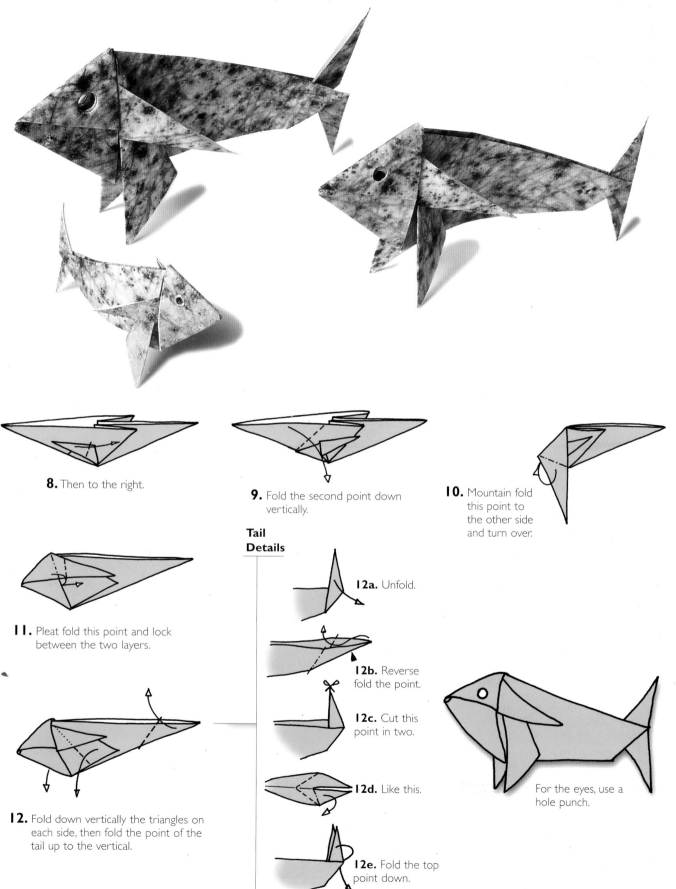

8. Then to the right.

9. Fold the second point down vertically.

10. Mountain fold this point to the other side and turn over.

Tail Details

11. Pleat fold this point and lock between the two layers.

12a. Unfold.

12b. Reverse fold the point.

12c. Cut this point in two.

12d. Like this.

12. Fold down vertically the triangles on each side, then fold the point of the tail up to the vertical.

12e. Fold the top point down.

For the eyes, use a hole punch.

Owl

▶ Beginner

How can an owl sleep with its eyes closed, perched on a branch many feet from the ground, without ever falling down? In fact, during the day owls most often rest in hollow trees, and at night they hoot and hunt in the moonlight.

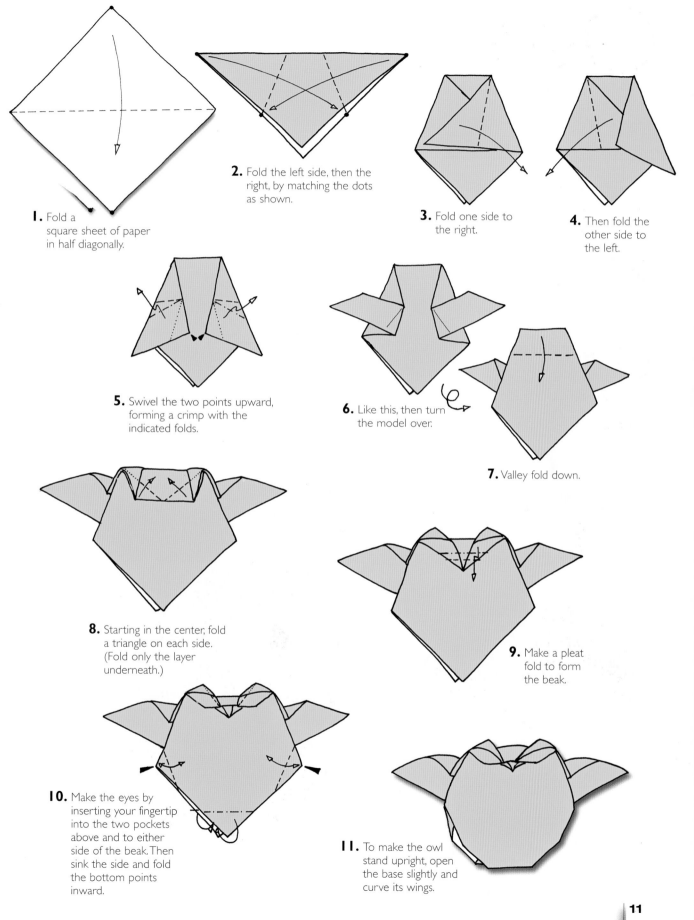

1. Fold a square sheet of paper in half diagonally.

2. Fold the left side, then the right, by matching the dots as shown.

3. Fold one side to the right.

4. Then fold the other side to the left.

5. Swivel the two points upward, forming a crimp with the indicated folds.

6. Like this, then turn the model over.

7. Valley fold down.

8. Starting in the center, fold a triangle on each side. (Fold only the layer underneath.)

9. Make a pleat fold to form the beak.

10. Make the eyes by inserting your fingertip into the two pockets above and to either side of the beak. Then sink the side and fold the bottom points inward.

11. To make the owl stand upright, open the base slightly and curve its wings.

Elephant

Elephants always live near a source of water for drinking and bathing. And they like to play in the water too, just like kids—making waves and splashing their playmates.

12

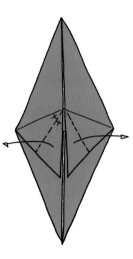

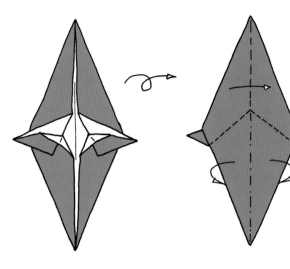

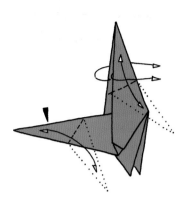

1. Start with the fish base (see p. 6). Bisect the angles as shown, folding the points to the outside.

2. While folding the points out, flatten the inner folds. Turn over.

3. Crease the diagonals, then fold in half on long vertical.

4. Outside reverse fold the upper point after prefolding (see p. 5). Inside reverse fold the left-hand point after prefolding.

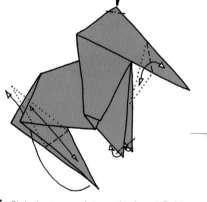

5. Sink the top point on the head. Fold and unfold trunk as shown. To form tail, inside reverse fold point on left. Outside reverse fold the front feet and spread the front legs.

Details

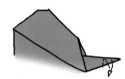

5a. Crimp fold the trunk.

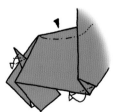

5b. Squash fold the tip.

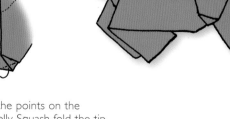

5c. Fold in the points on the elephant's belly. Squash fold the tip of the tail and round the back. To finish, shape the ears.

Heron

▶▶▶ Advanced

This superb wading bird with its big beak atop a long neck loves to have its feet in the water. A heron can stand for several hours on one leg while napping, with the other leg stretched out. To be sure your heron will stand up well, slip a small piece of wire between the folds of the feet.

1. Begin with the bird base (see p. 5). Fold one layer from the left side to the right.

2. Bring the uppermost lower point up and to the left, folding as shown.

3. Now fold one layer from the right side to the left.

4. Repeat Step 2 to the right.

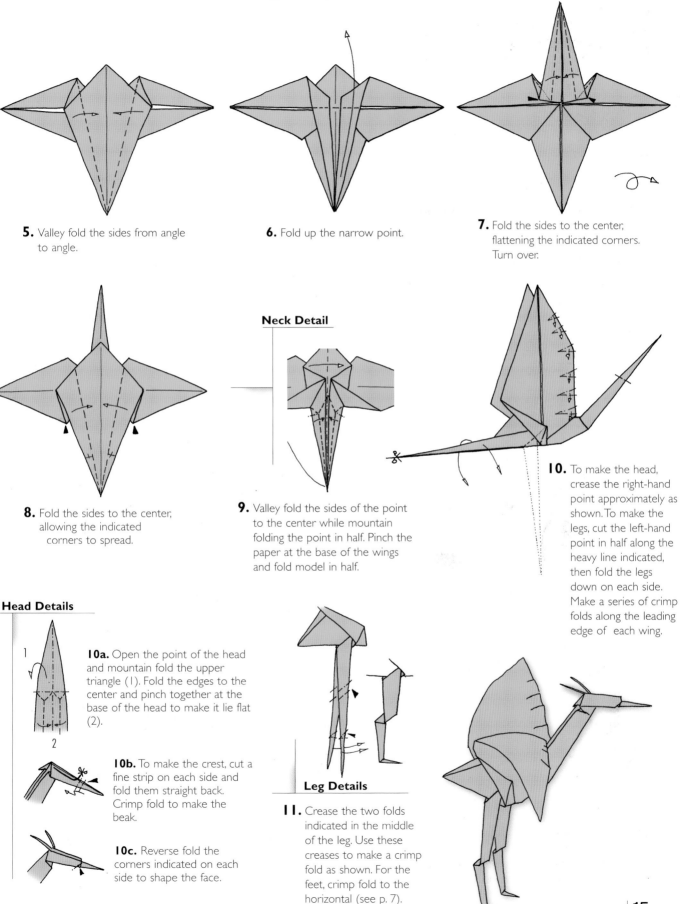

5. Valley fold the sides from angle to angle.

6. Fold up the narrow point.

7. Fold the sides to the center, flattening the indicated corners. Turn over.

Neck Detail

8. Fold the sides to the center, allowing the indicated corners to spread.

9. Valley fold the sides of the point to the center while mountain folding the point in half. Pinch the paper at the base of the wings and fold model in half.

10. To make the head, crease the right-hand point approximately as shown. To make the legs, cut the left-hand point in half along the heavy line indicated, then fold the legs down on each side. Make a series of crimp folds along the leading edge of each wing.

Head Details

10a. Open the point of the head and mountain fold the upper triangle (1). Fold the edges to the center and pinch together at the base of the head to make it lie flat (2).

10b. To make the crest, cut a fine strip on each side and fold them straight back. Crimp fold to make the beak.

10c. Reverse fold the corners indicated on each side to shape the face.

Leg Details

11. Crease the two folds indicated in the middle of the leg. Use these creases to make a crimp fold as shown. For the feet, crimp fold to the horizontal (see p. 7).

15

Penguin

▶▶ Intermediate

A penguin looks like a man in a
tuxedo when standing up, but its
waddling walk makes us laugh.
Penguins love to slide on the
ice and jump feet first into
the water.

1. Crease the diagonal of a
square sheet of paper.
Then fold the two
edges to the crease.

2. Fold in half to
the right.

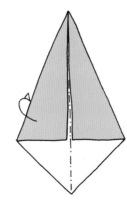 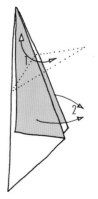 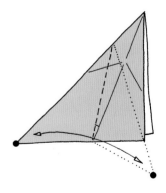

3. Fold the point as
shown. Then unfold the
head (1), and open the
sides out (2).

4. Crease by folding the
whole left side as shown,
then open completely.

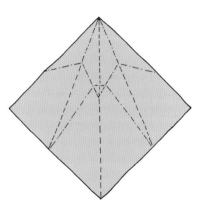

5. Before refolding, put the creases in mountain and valley folds, as shown.

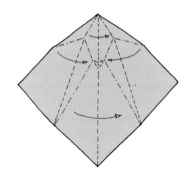

6. Begin to refold.

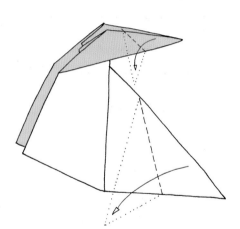

7. Fold the right point to the left. For the beak, valley fold the corner.

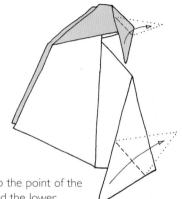

8. Bring up the point of the beak and the lower triangle, as shown.

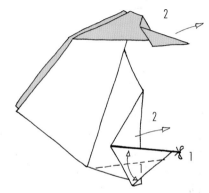

9. Cut on the solid line, crease at the base (1), and unfold the beak and the base (2).

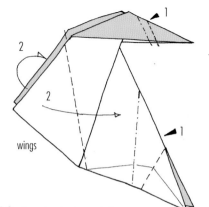

10. For the beak and the right point, open and make reverse folds (1). Valley fold the left side on each surface to make the wings (2).

Details

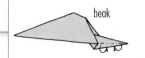

beak

10a. Make the beak narrower by folding half to the inside. Fold the tip.

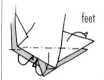

feet

10b. To bring out the feet, fold to the inside on existing creases. Then put the feet flat. Make the penguin three-dimensional from the inside.

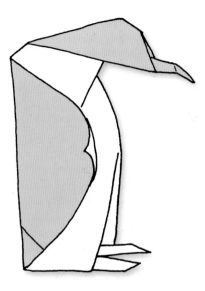

Dove

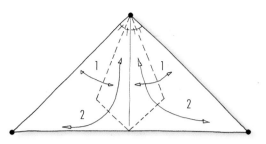

1. Starting with a half-square, precrease the edges to the vertical center fold (1), then crease the folds at the base by joining the end points to the apex (2).

▶▶ **Intermediate**

This white bird is often depicted in flight with an olive branch in its beak: a symbol of peace. You can suspend the dove by attaching nylon thread to each wing.

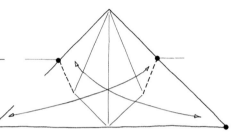

2. To make this crease, fold each point to the opposite edge making sure to keep the top edges horizontal.

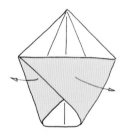

2a. Like this, then unfold.

3. Make reverse folds as shown, joining the points and using the existing creases.

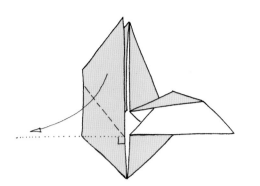

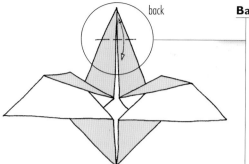

back

Back Details

5a. Fold the tip down using the existing creases, making the necessary valley to mountain fold adjustments, then close. Turn over.

4. Valley fold back the points to lie on the horizontal and flatten the interior folds.

5. Fold and unfold the upper point, then open this point.

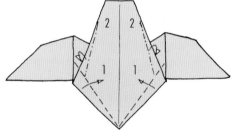

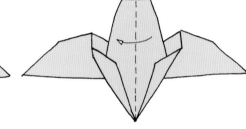

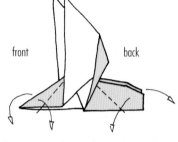

front   back

6. Valley fold the lower edges (1), then mountain fold the upper edges (2) to shape the body.

7. Fold in half.

8. At both the front and back, make outside reverse folds (see p. 5)

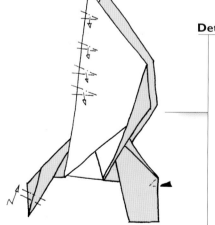

Details

head

9a. Inside reverse fold the corners on each side.

tail

9. Crimp fold the point of the head to form the beak. To curve the wings, make a series of small crimp folds.

9b. Push in the center of an imaginary triangle as shown to create volume.

Whether in town or in the countryside,
you're almost sure to find little songbirds.
Some of them fly thousands
of miles to find the sun.
Here you have two versions:
resting and flying.

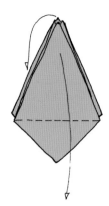

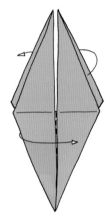

Bird

▷▷▷ Advanced

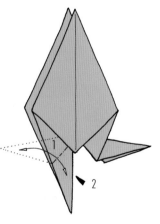

1. Start with a bird base (see p. 5) and fold down the front and rear flaps.

2. Fold the front left layer to the right and the right layer on the back to the left.

3. Reverse fold each point out to the horizontal.

Resting Bird

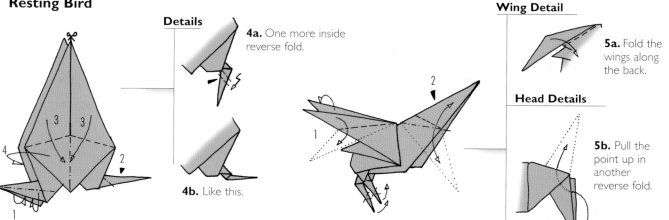

Details

4a. One more inside reverse fold.

4b. Like this.

Wing Detail

5a. Fold the wings along the back.

Head Details

5b. Pull the point up in another reverse fold.

5c. Bring the point down while opening the sides.

5d. Hold the point with your thumb and forefinger and tip up the point at the back of the head.

5e. Crimp fold to form beak (see p. 7).

5f. Thin the beak by folding the edges inside.

4. Start with the legs: narrow the two points by folding in half to the inside (1), then make inside reverse folds on each leg (2). Continue folding the legs by following Steps 4a and 4b. Cut the top flap in half along center crease, folding down the resulting two points (3). Fold the model in half along the center crease.

5. Fold the wings to lie along the back of the model (1). Crimp fold the legs to make the feet (see p. 7). Make a reverse fold for the head (2).

Flying Bird

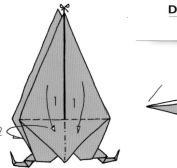

Details

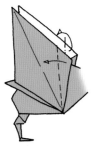

4a. Open each point (1) and squash fold vertically (2).

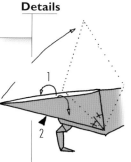

4b. Fold one side. Repeat on back.

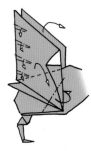

4c. Fold the lower corner under. Fold wing down along back of model and make a series of small crimp folds on the trailing edge to curve the wing. Repeat on the other side.

4. To make a bird with wings spread, cut the top point in half, then fold the wings (1). Mountain fold in half along vertical axis.

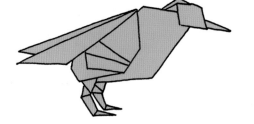

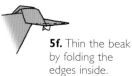

21

Hen...

In the farmyard, hens go about their business pecking at seeds, snapping at small insects, and sitting on their eggs.

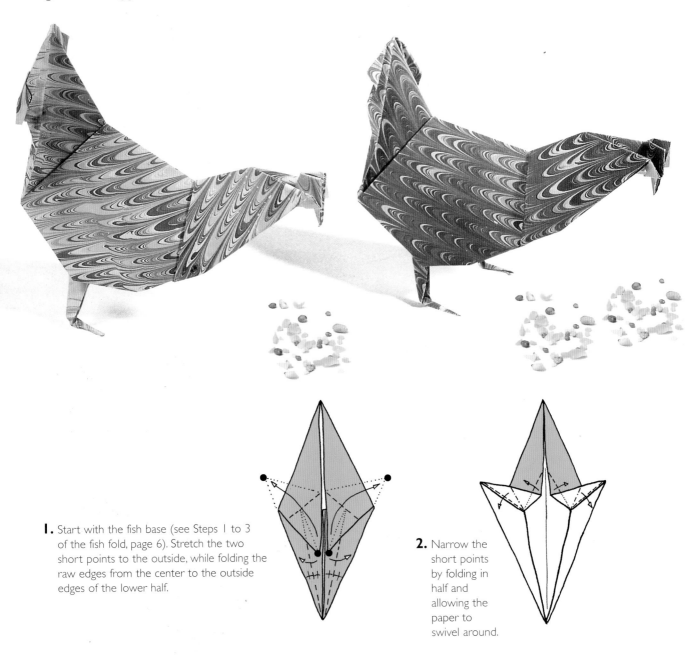

1. Start with the fish base (see Steps 1 to 3 of the fish fold, page 6). Stretch the two short points to the outside, while folding the raw edges from the center to the outside edges of the lower half.

2. Narrow the short points by folding in half and allowing the paper to swivel around.

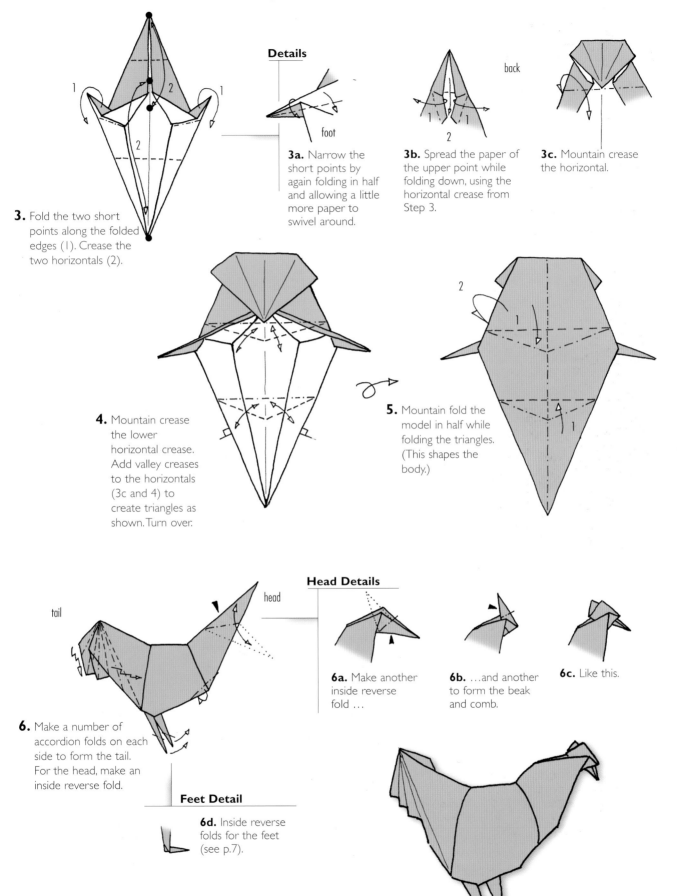

Details

3a. Narrow the short points by again folding in half and allowing a little more paper to swivel around.

foot

back

3b. Spread the paper of the upper point while folding down, using the horizontal crease from Step 3.

3c. Mountain crease the horizontal.

3. Fold the two short points along the folded edges (1). Crease the two horizontals (2).

4. Mountain crease the lower horizontal crease. Add valley creases to the horizontals (3c and 4) to create triangles as shown. Turn over.

5. Mountain fold the model in half while folding the triangles. (This shapes the body.)

tail

head

Head Details

6a. Make another inside reverse fold …

6b. …and another to form the beak and comb.

6c. Like this.

6. Make a number of accordion folds on each side to form the tail. For the head, make an inside reverse fold.

Feet Detail

6d. Inside reverse folds for the feet (see p.7).

...and the Chick

What came first, the chicken or the egg? A riddle as old as the world, which you can ponder while folding a chick that's just been hatched from its shell.

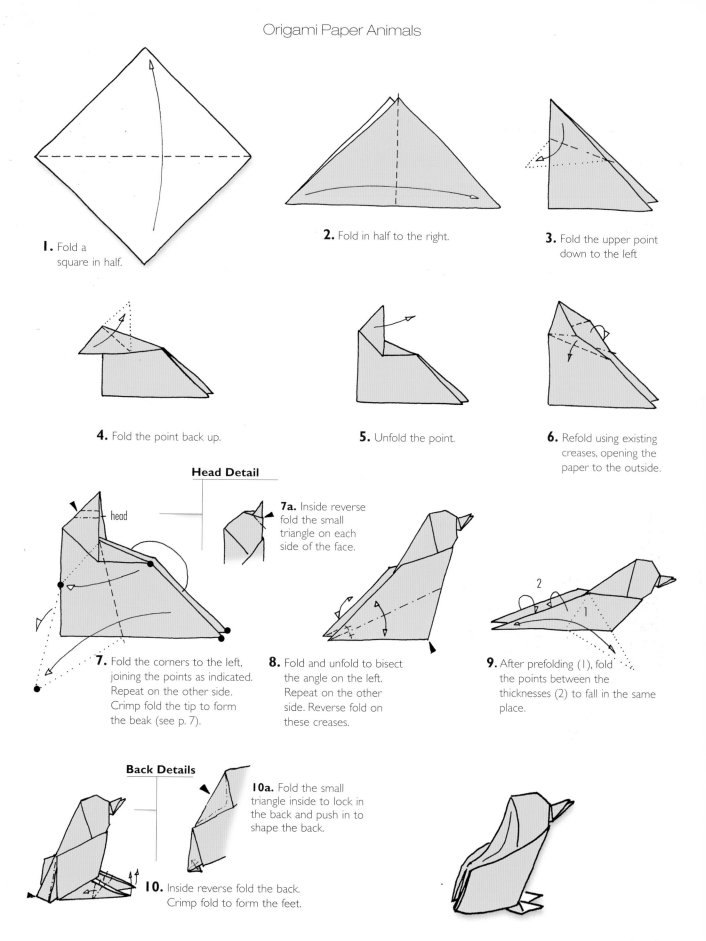

1. Fold a square in half.

2. Fold in half to the right.

3. Fold the upper point down to the left

4. Fold the point back up.

5. Unfold the point.

6. Refold using existing creases, opening the paper to the outside.

Head Detail

head

7a. Inside reverse fold the small triangle on each side of the face.

7. Fold the corners to the left, joining the points as indicated. Repeat on the other side. Crimp fold the tip to form the beak (see p. 7).

8. Fold and unfold to bisect the angle on the left. Repeat on the other side. Reverse fold on these creases.

9. After prefolding (1), fold the points between the thicknesses (2) to fall in the same place.

Back Details

10a. Fold the small triangle inside to lock in the back and push in to shape the back.

10. Inside reverse fold the back. Crimp fold to form the feet.

Panther

Intermediate

This feline, which looks like a big cat, owns several passports. In Africa his name is leopard, while in the Americas he is known as a jaguar. In Hollywood, he is a star, his long pink silhouette strolling elegantly in animated form.

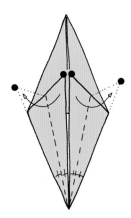

1. Start with a fish base (see p. 6). Open to the outside.

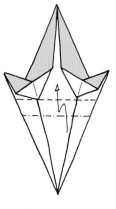

2. Pleat fold.

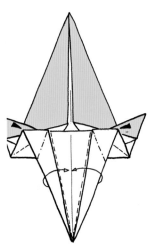

3. Narrow the lower point by folding the edges to the center fold and make it lie flat.

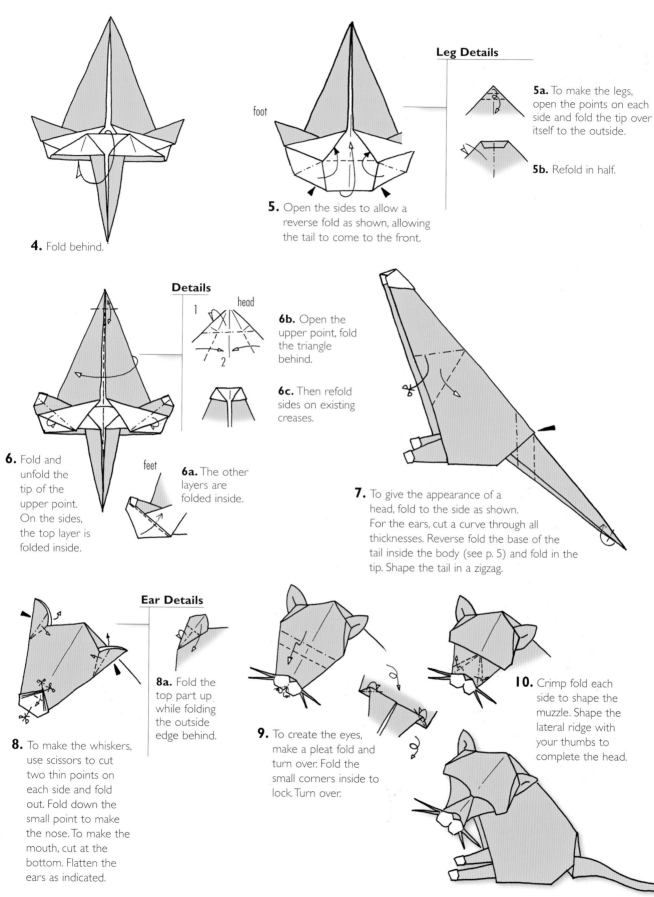

Leg Details

5a. To make the legs, open the points on each side and fold the tip over itself to the outside.

5b. Refold in half.

foot

5. Open the sides to allow a reverse fold as shown, allowing the tail to come to the front.

4. Fold behind.

Details

1

head

2

6b. Open the upper point, fold the triangle behind.

6c. Then refold sides on existing creases.

6. Fold and unfold the tip of the upper point. On the sides, the top layer is folded inside.

feet

6a. The other layers are folded inside.

7. To give the appearance of a head, fold to the side as shown. For the ears, cut a curve through all thicknesses. Reverse fold the base of the tail inside the body (see p. 5) and fold in the tip. Shape the tail in a zigzag.

Ear Details

8a. Fold the top part up while folding the outside edge behind.

8. To make the whiskers, use scissors to cut two thin points on each side and fold out. Fold down the small point to make the nose. To make the mouth, cut at the bottom. Flatten the ears as indicated.

9. To create the eyes, make a pleat fold and turn over. Fold the small corners inside to lock. Turn over.

10. Crimp fold each side to shape the muzzle. Shape the lateral ridge with your thumbs to complete the head.

Eagle

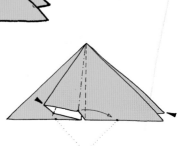

1. Starting with a waterbomb base (see p. 5), fold one point on each side down along the center crease, then unfold.

▶▶▶ Advanced

The eagle is a powerful and majestic raptor that soars on high, spotting prey with its sharp eyesight. It generally carries its catch between its talons several miles in the air. The eagle presented here can hold a small object between its feet or can balance on a finger.

2. Open the point and squash fold it symmetrically. Repeat on other side.

3. Make creases by folding edges to the central crease. Unfold and make them reverse folds.

4. Fold the resulting point up to meet the top point, flattening the model, then turn over.

5. Fold long edges to the central crease.

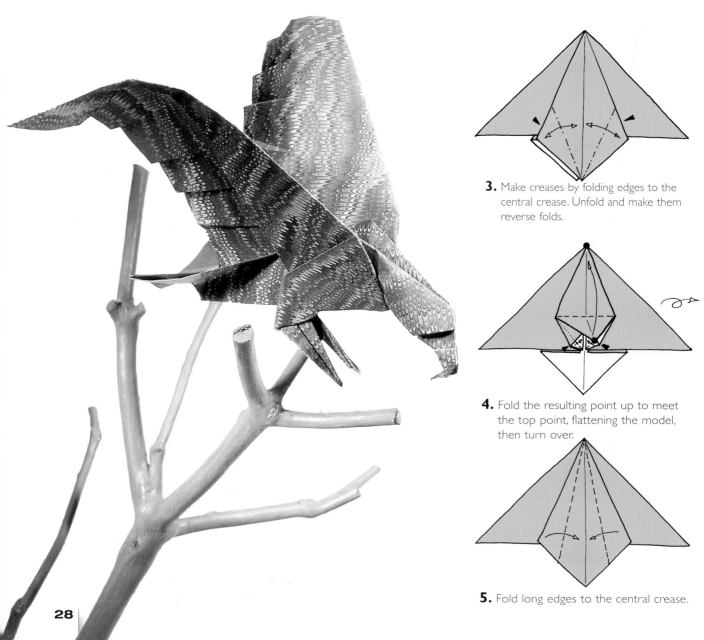

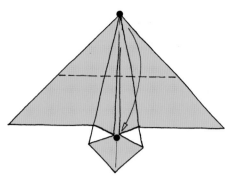

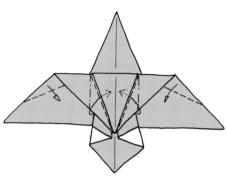

6. Fold upper point down, as indicated.

7. Fold the top of the wings as indicated and slide the folds between the thicknesses of the central triangle.

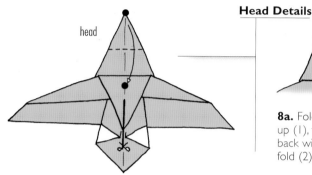

head

Head Details

8a. Fold the point back up (1), then flip it to the back with a small crimp fold (2).

8b. Fold the sides and turn over.

8c. Fold the triangle up to shape the beak.

8. To make the legs, cut along the heavy line through all thicknesses of the triangle. To make the head, fold the upper point down as shown.

Tail Details

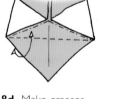

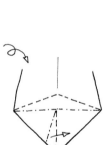

8d. Make creases as indicated, then turn over.

8e. Pleat fold to make it three-dimensional.

8f. To lock in the fold, tuck in the triangle between the layers.

9. Fold the upper edges under, fold the excess paper on the wings under, and fold the model in half.

10. Open the back and shape with two folds. Fold the legs to the inside and finish the hook in the beak with an inside reverse fold (see p. 5)

11. Slide your index finger inside the edge of the wings: it's ready to fly.

Whale

▶ Beginner

A whale can jump out of the water gracefully despite its weight, which can exceed 150 tons. In some species of whales, their teeth are replaced by numerous plates that filter the plankton and tiny fish that make up their diet. We hope that this fold will make you laugh like a whale.

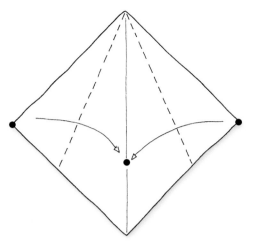

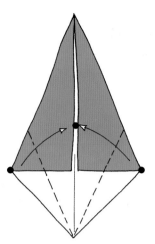

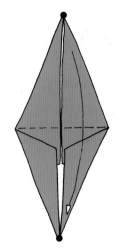

1. Starting with a square, creased on the diagonal, fold the edges to the center crease.

2. Fold the other two edges to the center.

3. Fold the top point to the bottom.

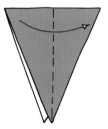

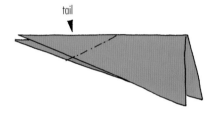

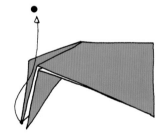

4. Fold in two.

5. Make a reverse fold after precreasing.

6. Bring one point back up with a small reverse fold.

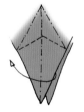

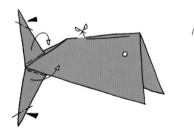

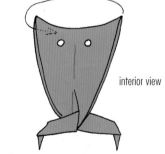

7. Detail of the folding of the point of the tail.

8. Make small reverse folds on the tips of the tail. Cut a thin strip along the back, and fold straight up, spreading to look like a water jet. For the eyes, paper punch through all thicknesses. Turn over.

9. Round the body and tuck one side into the other.

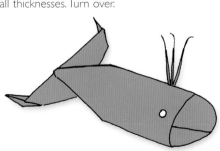

Cat

)))) Advanced

The cat is the domesticated member of the feline family. It seeks out human companionship now and again and even lets itself be stroked when it feels like it. Then, as if on a whim, it runs away a moment later.

Body

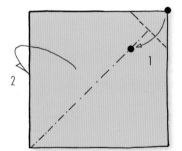

1. Start with a square slightly larger than the one you will use for the head. With the color side up, valley fold a small corner down (1), then mountain fold in two along the diagonal (2).

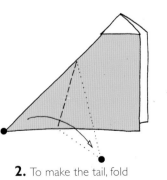

2. To make the tail, fold the point down.

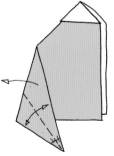

3. Fold the point in half (1), then unfold (2).

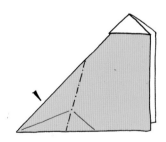

4. Reverse fold on existing crease.

32

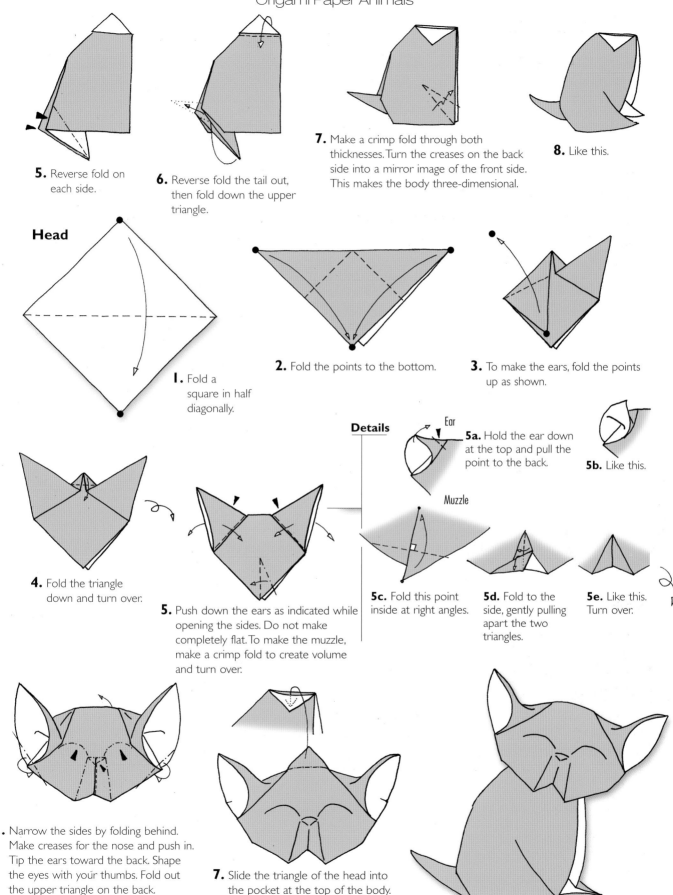

5. Reverse fold on each side.

6. Reverse fold the tail out, then fold down the upper triangle.

7. Make a crimp fold through both thicknesses. Turn the creases on the back side into a mirror image of the front side. This makes the body three-dimensional.

8. Like this.

Head

1. Fold a square in half diagonally.

2. Fold the points to the bottom.

3. To make the ears, fold the points up as shown.

4. Fold the triangle down and turn over.

5. Push down the ears as indicated while opening the sides. Do not make completely flat. To make the muzzle, make a crimp fold to create volume and turn over.

Details

Ear

5a. Hold the ear down at the top and pull the point to the back.

5b. Like this.

Muzzle

5c. Fold this point inside at right angles.

5d. Fold to the side, gently pulling apart the two triangles.

5e. Like this. Turn over.

. Narrow the sides by folding behind. Make creases for the nose and push in. Tip the ears toward the back. Shape the eyes with your thumbs. Fold out the upper triangle on the back.

7. Slide the triangle of the head into the pocket at the top of the body.

33

Horse

▶▶ Intermediate

The horse is the most beautiful of man's conquests—as every equestrian will agree. To make this horse stand on its hind legs, all you need to do is fold the points again and find the balance point.

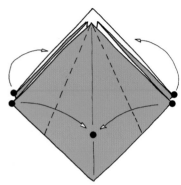

1. Fold in the sides of a preliminary base (see p. 5).

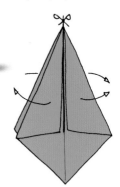

2. Cut along the heavy line only as far as the folded edge, then unfold.

3. Fold down the points on both sides, front and back.

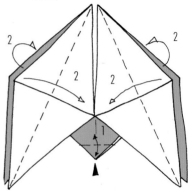

4. Sink the base after prefolding (1) (see p. 6). Fold the sides along the existing creases (2).

back **head**

5. Mark the position of the head as the dotted line indicates and precrease the tail: one fold at right angles and a second fold dividing the resulting angle in half.

6. To make the mane, cut a point through all thicknesses; for the ears, cut a curve through all thicknesses.

Head Details

7. Open the head and make a pleat fold to create nostrils.

8. Stand the ears up (1) before refolding the head with a reverse fold (2).

9. Make a reverse fold to form the mouth.

10. Like this.

Back Details

11. Open the point to form the back, then push down inside the folds on each side.

12. Make a pleat fold to the inside to form the tail.

Tail Details

13. Make a reverse fold.

14. Open to the outside.

15. Narrow the base of the tail and shape the tip with a reverse fold.

16. For a trotting horse, make a reverse fold on one front leg and on the opposite rear leg. Tip the head forward with a crimp fold on each side. To finish, give it a little volume.

Dog

▶▶ Intermediate

This dog resembles a fox because of his square muzzle and pointed ears—but you can count on him to risk his life to save his master. This dog knows how to rest quietly, but he certainly has plenty of personality.

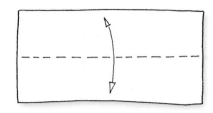

1. Mark the center fold of a rectangle 1 × 2 (a half-square).

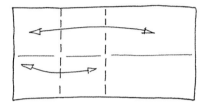

2. Mark the half, then the quarter.

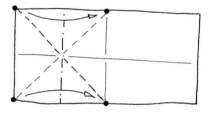

3. Fold the diagonals, then make a water-bomb base (see p. 5)

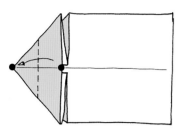

4. Open up by joining the points.

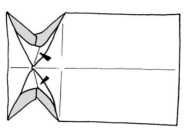

5. Flatten completely.

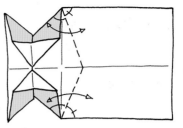

6. Precrease by dividing the angle in half, then turn over.

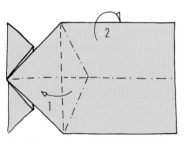

7. Valley fold on the vertical crease while mountain folding the diagonal creases (1). This will collapse the small triangle. Mountain fold along the central crease (2). These folds occur as one movement.

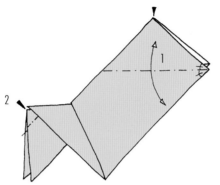

8. Make a reverse fold after precreasing the angle in half (1). Reverse fold the small corner (on the left) to indicate the tail (2).

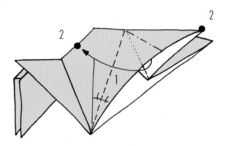

9. Open and fold down the top thickness of paper to the vertical line (1). The model will naturally lie flat on joining the points (2). Repeat on the other side.

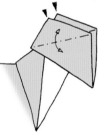

10. Make a reverse fold after precreasing for the ears.

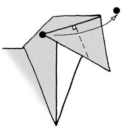

11. Fold a right angle as shown and press the point of the ear flat. Repeat on the other ear.

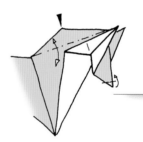

12. For the nose, fold back the point and open slightly. On the top, make a precrease before sinking the point as shown.

Neck Details

12a. Find the indicated creases and push inside. If this is too difficult, simply fold the triangle of the neck back to the previous step.

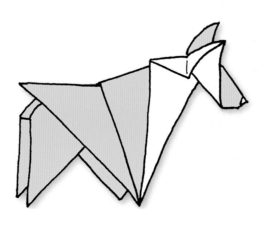

Crab

▶▶▶ Advanced

This familiar crustacean from the seashore has a pair of large pincers used for self-defense…and sometimes to taste your big toes! Its sideways walk gives the impression that it is running away on tiptoes.

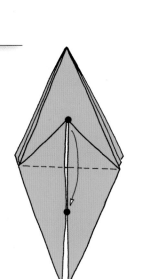

1. Start with a frog base (see p. 6) and fold down the small points on each side.

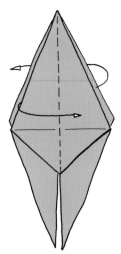

2. Fold over two thicknesses on each side to expose two new triangles.

3. Fold the point along the horizontal and unfold.

4. Using the creases from Step 3, open the side slightly and slide the whole point to the left, as shown on the right.

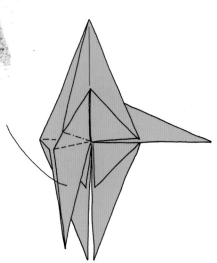

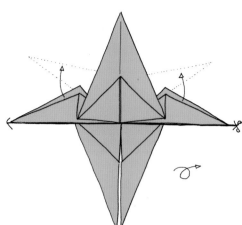

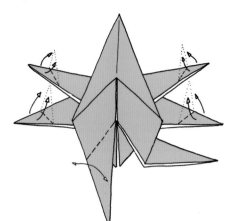

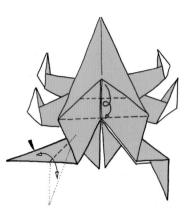

5. To double the number of legs, cut the center fold of both points in two. Slide the rearmost points toward the top (indicated by dotted line). Turn over.

6. On the four upper legs, make outside reverse folds (see p. 5) after prefolding and turning the tips out. On the lower points, precrease, then reverse fold as shown on the right.

7. Make another inside reverse fold (see p. 5) on these smaller points as on the right.

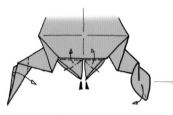

Details

8a. Like this.

8b. Fold over the sides of these squares to form the eyes.

pincer

8c. Turn the entire fold inside out like this.

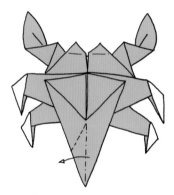

8. To make the pincers, fold over one thickness and flip the end inside as on the right (8c). For the eyes, fold back the triangles, then open and flatten the resulting squares.

9. Crimp fold the point to the left to make the shell hollow.

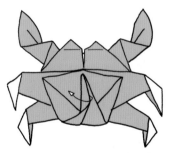

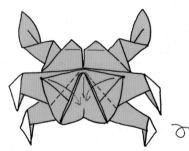

10. Fold the point to the top.

11. Open the left side of this point.

12. To lock in shape, tuck loose points between the layers of the center triangle. Turn over.

Giraffe

▶▶ Intermediate

At about 18 feet high, the giraffe is the tallest animal alive. Although mute, its excellent vision allows it to see any potential enemy from afar. To drink is extremely difficult since it must do leg splits to get its head down in the water.

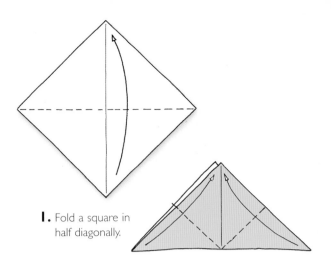

1. Fold a square in half diagonally.

2. Fold up both points.

3. Fold the sides to the center, then unfold.

4. Cut two slits for the tail.

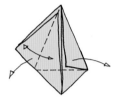

4a. Cut across one thickness only and unfold strip for tail.

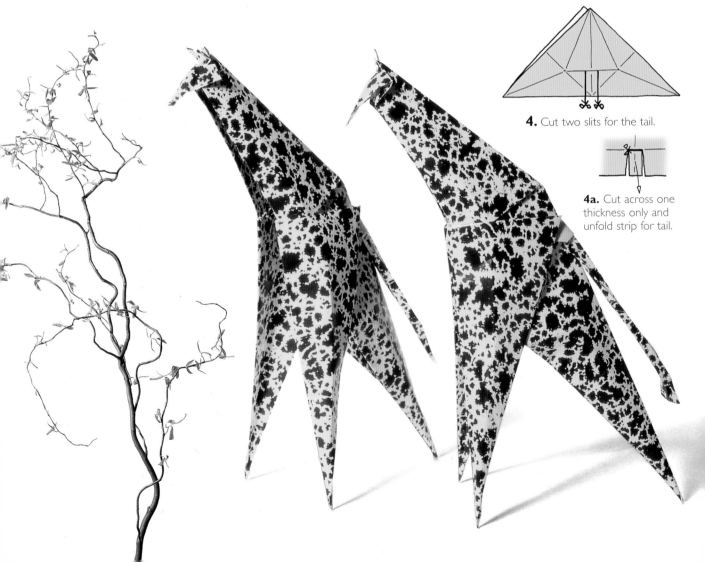

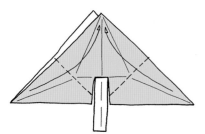

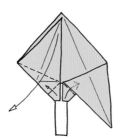

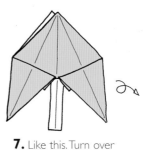

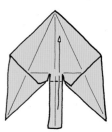

5. Fold the points to the top.

6. Valley fold the two points down to the top of the slit for the tail as shown on the right, and fold the small flaps under.

7. Like this. Turn over

8. Fold up the tail.

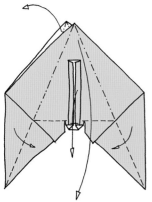

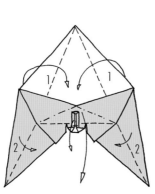

Tail Details

9. Open the two layers, folding the top layer toward the front.

10. At the same time, refold the sides on the existing creases (1) and fold the lower points in two to make the model lie flat.

8a. Fold the sides to the center crease and make the small triangle at the bottom flat, as on the left.

8b. Like this.

11. Fold in two.

12. Make crimp folds on both sides and tuck under the layers of the leg as shown.

Head Details

14a. Fold in corners of muzzle and flatten the head a little.

14b. Like this.

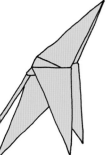

13. Like this.

14. Crimp fold to place head (1). Cut the ears and the horns, then separate and cut on the center fold (2). Fold in the tip of the point (3), then finish the fold for the head.

Tail Details

14c. Fold the sides up on the long diagonal.

14d. Fold out the bottom end of each side.

14e. Like this. Gently curve the tail and shape the body and neck.

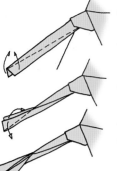

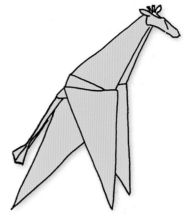

Rabbit

In the wild, rabbits live in family groups deep under the earth in burrows they have dug themselves. Its acute hearing, thanks to big ears, alerts it to danger. Then it bolts as fast as possible, jumping in a zigzag pattern to throw off the enemy.

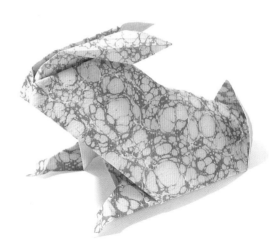

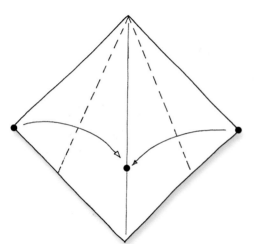

1. Fold the sides to the center crease.

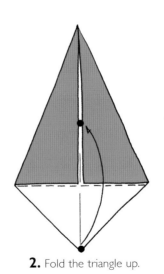

2. Fold the triangle up.

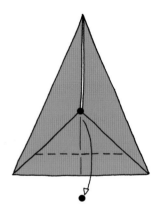

3. Fold the tip back down, joining the points.

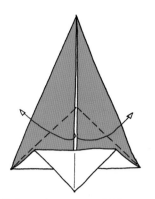

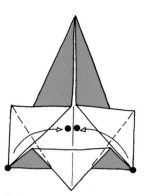

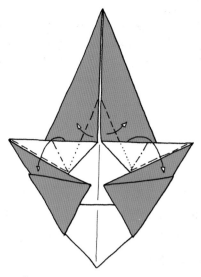

4. Pull out the corners, folding them along the edge of the preceding fold.

5. Fold in the sides as shown.

6. To narrow the points, fold down one layer and open along marked folds.

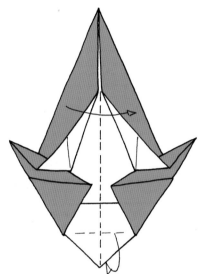

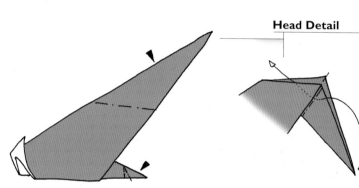

Head Detail

7. Bend the bottom point to the back to make the tail, then fold model in half along the vertical.

8. After precreasing, reverse fold the large point. For the feet, make squash folds as for the ears (Steps 11 and 12). Loosen the tail and shape the body.

9. Inside reverse fold.

Ear Details

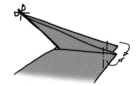

10. Cut the point in two to separate the ears. Fold the tips at the front inside, sliding one inside the other to form the muzzle.

11. Squash fold.

12. Like this. Shape the ears, then the back, to give your rabbit volume.

Dragonfly

▶▶ Intermediate

The dragonfly, which is also called the damselfly, has four transparent wings as delicate as lace. In flight, the buzzing of the wings sounds like a helicopter's blades in the air. Sometimes dragonflies enjoy performing aerial acrobatics just above water level.

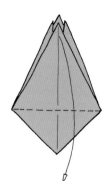

1. Starting with a bird base (see p. 5), fold one point down.

2. Fold the two points vertically, then open and flatten evenly (squash fold) as on the right.

3. Like this, then turn over.

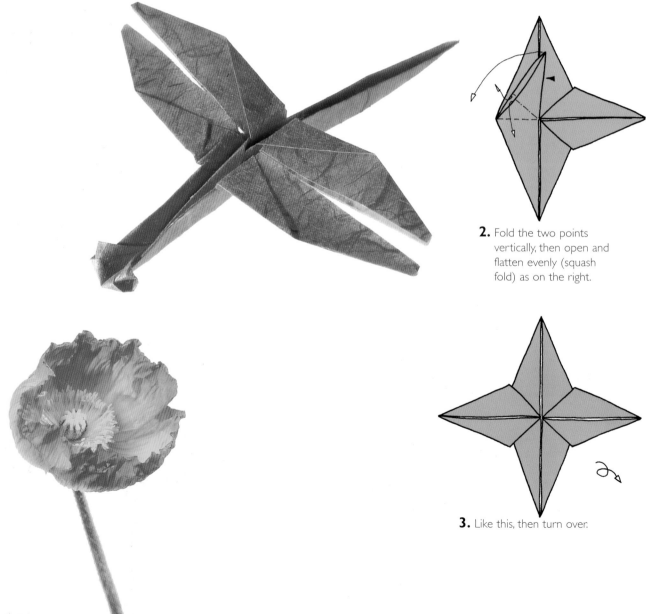

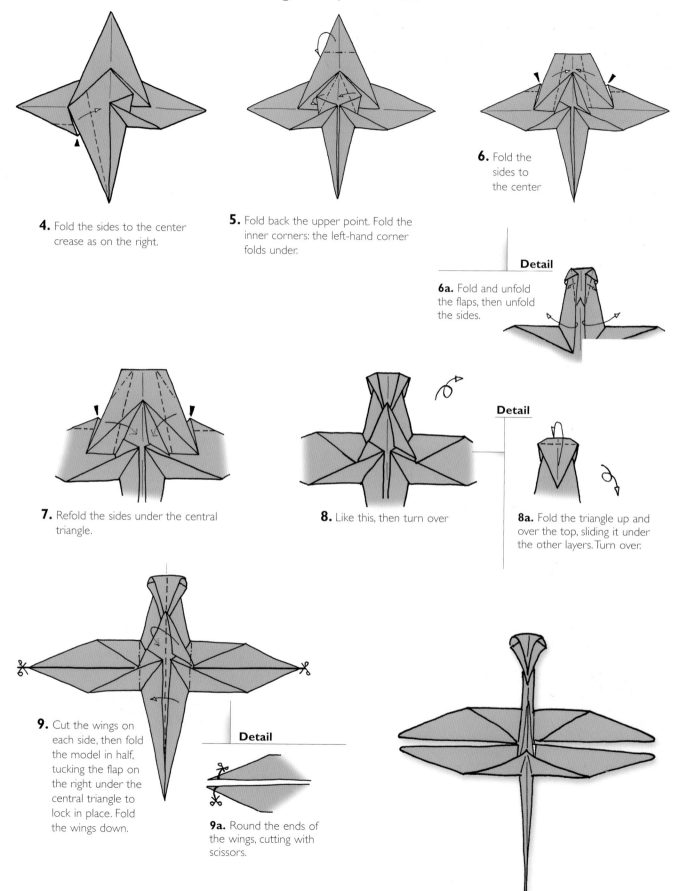

4. Fold the sides to the center crease as on the right.

5. Fold back the upper point. Fold the inner corners: the left-hand corner folds under.

6. Fold the sides to the center

Detail

6a. Fold and unfold the flaps, then unfold the sides.

7. Refold the sides under the central triangle.

8. Like this, then turn over

Detail

8a. Fold the triangle up and over the top, sliding it under the other layers. Turn over.

9. Cut the wings on each side, then fold the model in half, tucking the flap on the right under the central triangle to lock in place. Fold the wings down.

Detail

9a. Round the ends of the wings, cutting with scissors.

Frog

▶▶▶ Advanced

Frogs love to congregate at the edges of ponds at nightfall to organize croaking concerts that herald rain and sometimes fine weather. Their fingertips act like suction cups, allowing them to climb anywhere without falling down.

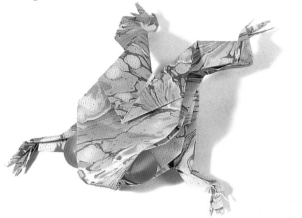

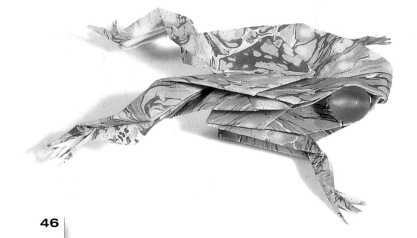

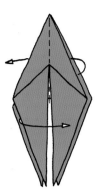

1. Start with the frog base (see p. 6) and fold over one layer on each side.

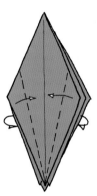

2. Fold the edges to the center on each side.

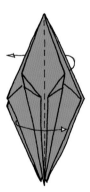

3. Fold over layers on each side to find sides that look like Step 2, and fold the sides in as in Step 2 on both sides.

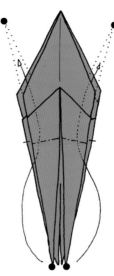

4. Fold over one layer on each side.

5. To make the front legs, reverse fold the points of the upper layer to the front.

6. To make the rear legs, make inside reverse folds (see p. 5) as on the left.

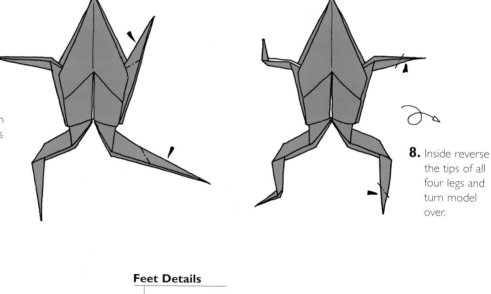

7. Make reverse folds in front and rear legs as shown on the left.

8. Inside reverse the tips of all four legs and turn model over.

9. You need to stop here and inflate the frog from the rear. You can also add beads between the layers as shown for eyes and fold the front tip under. Finally, cut the tips of the legs in half.

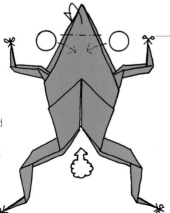

Feet Details

9a. Then open the tips of the legs to cut the points again to make five toes.

Sheep

Sheep are very gentle animals with a thick coat of wool.
They bleat as they play, jumping in the air. The work of a
flock of sheep is to mow a meadow in record time—
without ever lifting up their heads from their jobs.

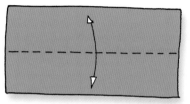

1. Crease the center line of a rectangle 1 × 2 (a half-square) color side up.

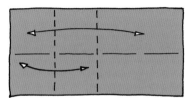

2. Crease the half and then the quarter.

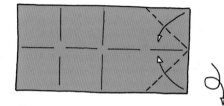

3. Fold the corners to the center crease, then turn over.

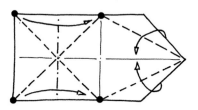

4. Crease the diagonals on the left side to make a water-bomb base (see p. 5). On the right side, fold as indicated bringing around the paper from behind.

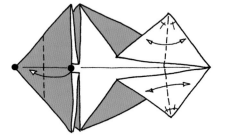

5. Open the left side by joining the dots; on the right side, crease to divide the angles in half.

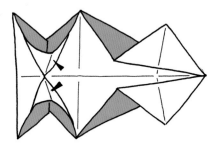

6. Flatten the left side.

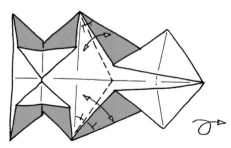

7. Mark the creases that divide the indicated angles and turn over.

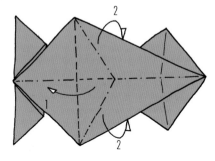

8. Valley fold on the vertical crease while mountain folding the diagonal creases (1). This will collapse the small triangle. Mountain fold along the central crease (2). These folds occur as one movement.

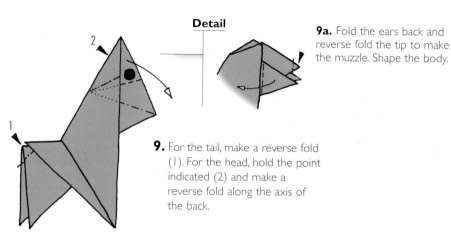

Detail

9a. Fold the ears back and reverse fold the tip to make the muzzle. Shape the body.

9. For the tail, make a reverse fold (1). For the head, hold the point indicated (2) and make a reverse fold along the axis of the back.

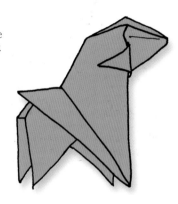

Parrot

▶▶ Intermediate

Parrots are appreciated not only for their magnificent plumage, but also for their ability to reproduce numerous sounds and words in all languages. Fold your parrot from colorful paper or a flyer. The only thing missing is speech, but parrots learn very quickly.

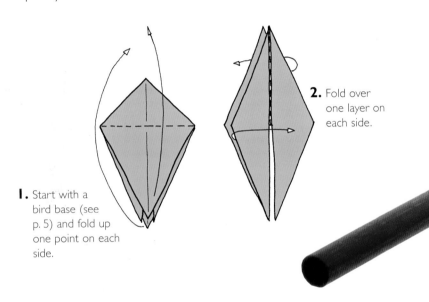

2. Fold over one layer on each side.

1. Start with a bird base (see p. 5) and fold up one point on each side.

Leg Detail

5a. Fold the point to the left and repeat Steps 4 and 5 on the right.

3. Cut through all layers along the heavy line, then fold one layer back on each side as in previous step.

4. Precrease the two lower points on the horizontal. Lift the left side vertically, open and push it down to lie flat.

5. Fold and unfold the sides to the center crease, then make reverse folds.

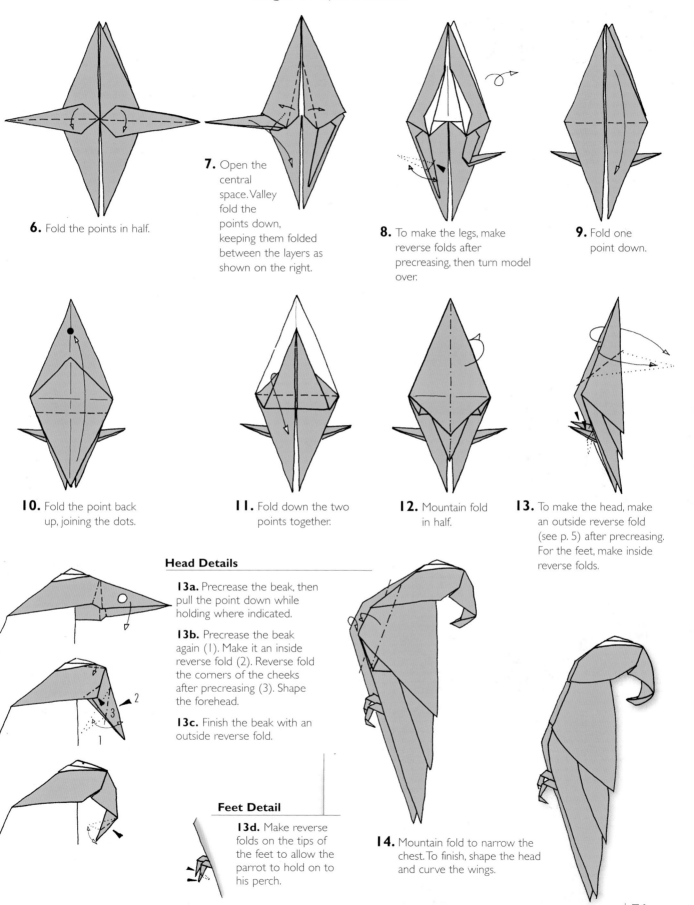

6. Fold the points in half.

7. Open the central space. Valley fold the points down, keeping them folded between the layers as shown on the right.

8. To make the legs, make reverse folds after precreasing, then turn model over.

9. Fold one point down.

10. Fold the point back up, joining the dots.

11. Fold down the two points together.

12. Mountain fold in half.

13. To make the head, make an outside reverse fold (see p. 5) after precreasing. For the feet, make inside reverse folds.

Head Details

13a. Precrease the beak, then pull the point down while holding where indicated.

13b. Precrease the beak again (1). Make it an inside reverse fold (2). Reverse fold the corners of the cheeks after precreasing (3). Shape the forehead.

13c. Finish the beak with an outside reverse fold.

Feet Detail

13d. Make reverse folds on the tips of the feet to allow the parrot to hold on to his perch.

14. Mountain fold to narrow the chest. To finish, shape the head and curve the wings.

Seal

▶ Beginner

The seal has an inner sense of balance that makes it a natural circus performer juggling balls. Seals usually live in cold polar waters, feeding on fish. At the end of the day when they are tired, they like to float on their sides.

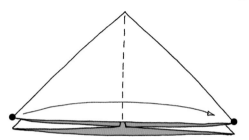

1. Start with a water-bomb base (see p. 5) with color inside. Fold one side to the right.

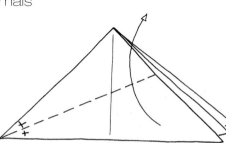

2. Fold the triangle up along the left edge bisecting the angle.

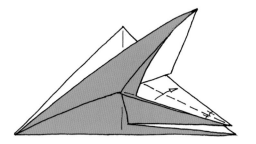

3. Then flatten the second layer to lie along the right-hand edge.

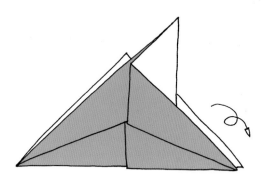

4. Like this, then turn over.

5. Repeat Steps 2 to 4 on the other side.

6. Fold the top points down as shown, joining the dots, and cut the point on the left about 1 inch. Rotate the model.

7. Fold the tips between the layers (1), then fold the upper point to the right for the head (2).

Head Details

7b. Completely unfold the point.

7c. Fold the tip over to create the nose (1). Cut the sides to form the whiskers (2), then refold the head on the folds as indicated.

Detail

7a. Detail of the tail.

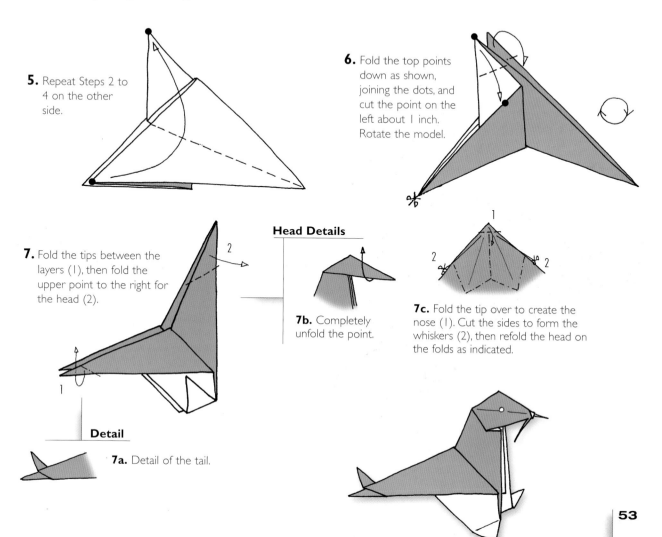

Grasshopper

The grasshopper, found in fields and meadows in summer, owes its name to the amazing jumps it makes when it extends its hind legs. Enjoy yourself as you create a life-sized creature.

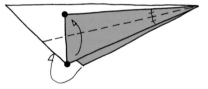

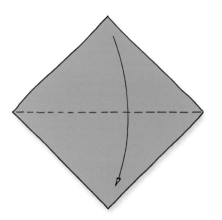

I. Mountain fold a square in half diagonally.

2. Fold the two sides upward on the diagonal as shown, joining the dots and leaving a bit of space from the upper edge.

3. Fold the two sides upward once more.

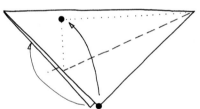

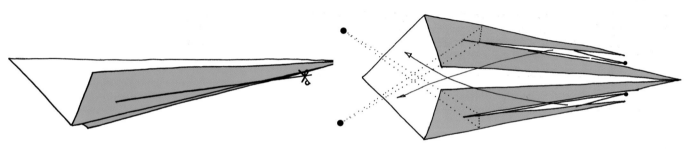

4. Cut a very fine strip in all layers.

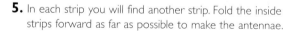

5. In each strip you will find another strip. Fold the inside strips forward as far as possible to make the antennae.

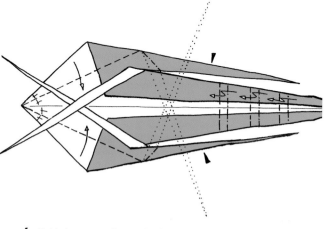

6. Fold the two other strips in a reverse fold (see p. 5) after prefolding. On the left side, fold the edges toward the center. On the right side, make a series of pleat folds.

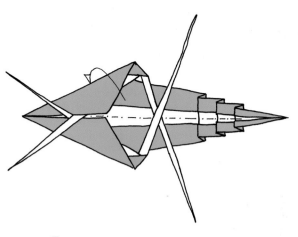

7. Mountain fold the model in half.

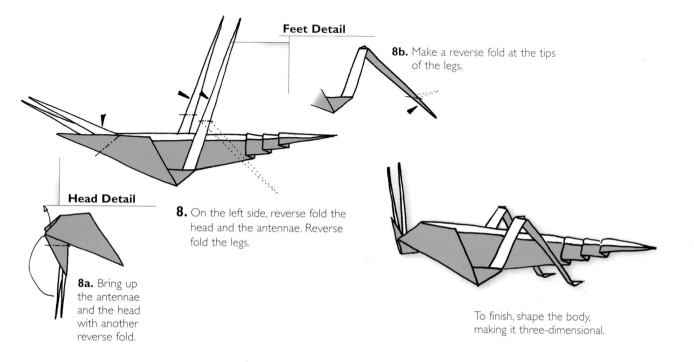

Feet Detail

8b. Make a reverse fold at the tips of the legs.

Head Detail

8. On the left side, reverse fold the head and the antennae. Reverse fold the legs.

8a. Bring up the antennae and the head with another reverse fold.

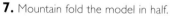

To finish, shape the body, making it three-dimensional.

Mouse

▶▶ Intermediate

When the cat's away, the mice will play. They're
especially fond of playing on attic floors while they
nibble grain—and nothing makes them happier
than a chunk of nippy cheese.

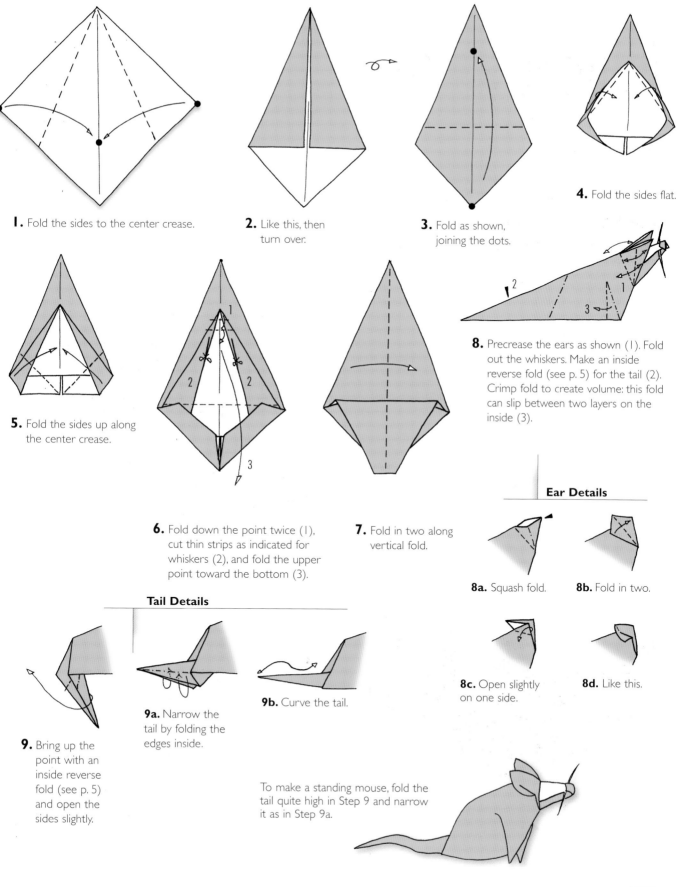

1. Fold the sides to the center crease.

2. Like this, then turn over.

3. Fold as shown, joining the dots.

4. Fold the sides flat.

5. Fold the sides up along the center crease.

6. Fold down the point twice (1), cut thin strips as indicated for whiskers (2), and fold the upper point toward the bottom (3).

7. Fold in two along vertical fold.

8. Precrease the ears as shown (1). Fold out the whiskers. Make an inside reverse fold (see p. 5) for the tail (2). Crimp fold to create volume: this fold can slip between two layers on the inside (3).

Ear Details

8a. Squash fold.

8b. Fold in two.

8c. Open slightly on one side.

8d. Like this.

Tail Details

9. Bring up the point with an inside reverse fold (see p. 5) and open the sides slightly.

9a. Narrow the tail by folding the edges inside.

9b. Curve the tail.

To make a standing mouse, fold the tail quite high in Step 9 and narrow it as in Step 9a.

Bull

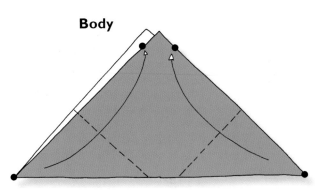

▶▶▶ Advanced

Throughout the centuries and in many civilizations, the bull has been revered for his strength. In Roman times, he enlivened the circus games, a custom that continues to this day in the south of France and in Spain. The bull you find here is quite harmless.

1. Fold a square (slightly larger than the one for the head) in half diagonally, then fold the points up leaving a space as shown.

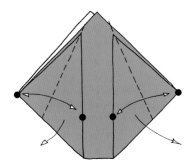

2. Fold through all layers while folding the points in two. Unfold.

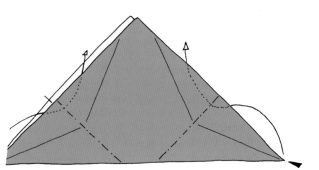

3. Make reverse folds on both sides.

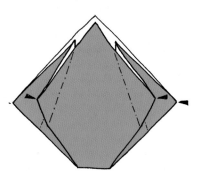

4. Following existing creases, make reverse folds on the four corners.

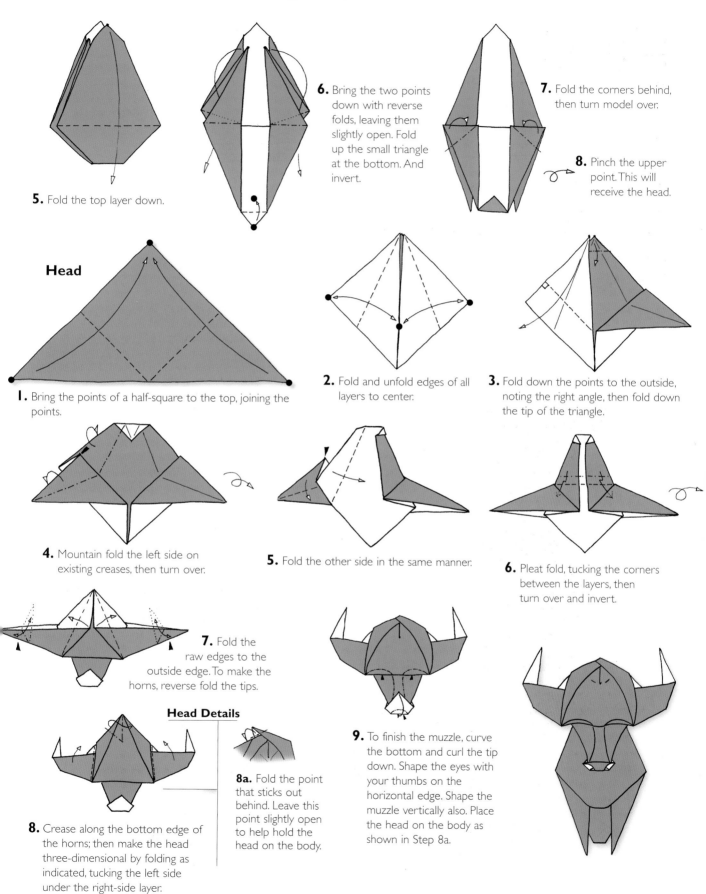

5. Fold the top layer down.

6. Bring the two points down with reverse folds, leaving them slightly open. Fold up the small triangle at the bottom. And invert.

7. Fold the corners behind, then turn model over.

8. Pinch the upper point. This will receive the head.

Head

1. Bring the points of a half-square to the top, joining the points.

2. Fold and unfold edges of all layers to center.

3. Fold down the points to the outside, noting the right angle, then fold down the tip of the triangle.

4. Mountain fold the left side on existing creases, then turn over.

5. Fold the other side in the same manner.

6. Pleat fold, tucking the corners between the layers, then turn over and invert.

7. Fold the raw edges to the outside edge. To make the horns, reverse fold the tips.

Head Details

8. Crease along the bottom edge of the horns; then make the head three-dimensional by folding as indicated, tucking the left side under the right-side layer.

8a. Fold the point that sticks out behind. Leave this point slightly open to help hold the head on the body.

9. To finish the muzzle, curve the bottom and curl the tip down. Shape the eyes with your thumbs on the horizontal edge. Shape the muzzle vertically also. Place the head on the body as shown in Step 8a.

Turtle

▶ Beginner

Turtles can grow up to 8 feet and can weigh up to 650 pounds. More at home in water than on land, turtles swim well because of their long, flattened, fin-like feet. What is most admired is the beauty of the carapace, which varies in color and pattern from one species to another. Now it's up to you to decorate your turtle. Let your imagination go wild.

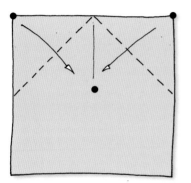

1. Starting with a square, color side up, crease the center vertically as shown. Fold the corners down along this crease, joining the dots.

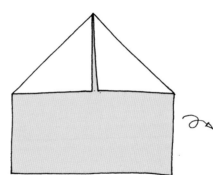

2. Like this, then turn over.

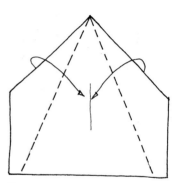

3. Fold the edges to the center crease, allowing the corners from behind to flip to the front.

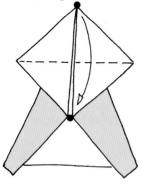

4. Fold the square in half.

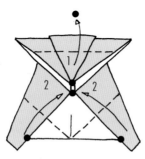

5. Fold up a third by joining the points (1), then fold the bottom edges along the vertical axis (2).

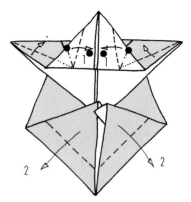

6. To form the front legs, join the points noting the fold lines (1) while narrowing the head. Then fold back the back legs (2).

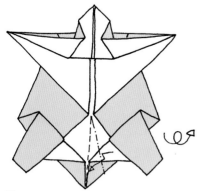

7. Add volume to the shell with a crimp fold, then turn over.

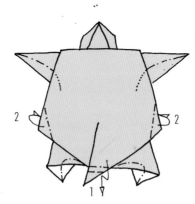

8. Make a pleat fold in the tail to lock in the back fold (1), then shape the legs and the head. To round the shell, fold under the corners on the sides (2).

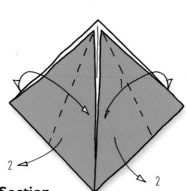

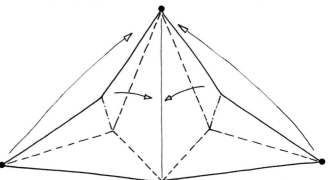

Upper Section

1. Fold up the points of a half-square (see Step 1 of the lower section), starting with the color side down. Next fold the edges to the center fold (1), then unfold completely (2).

Monkey

▶▶▶ Advanced

Monkeys have numerous human characteristics. Often making a spectacle of themselves by leaping acrobatically from branch to branch, they enjoy making children laugh by putting on funny faces and fooling around.

2. Fold the points back to the top, noting the direction of the folds.

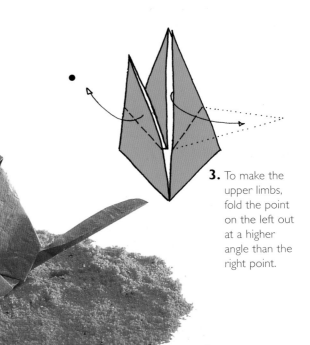

3. To make the upper limbs, fold the point on the left out at a higher angle than the right point.

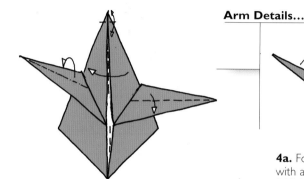

Arm Details... | **Muzzle Details**

4b - 4c. To make the muzzle, open the upper point, fold the triangle behind, then refold along the creases indicated.

4a. Fold the left arm up with an outside reverse fold (see p. 5)

(see p. 5)

4. Narrow the arms by folding in half, mountain fold on the left, and valley fold on the right. Fold and unfold the upper point. Follow Steps 4a through 4c, then fold the model in half.

5. To make the head, fold to the side, open, and push down the top.

6. Reverse fold the tip of the base (1). To make the ears, crimp with reverse folds (2). For the muzzle, fold the triangle (3).

7. To create the eyes, fold the triangle shown (1). For the muzzle, crimp on each side (2). Curve the muzzle (3).

Hand Details

5a. Open the upper limb, make the folds as indicated, then refold in two.

5b. Open the other arm, make the folds as indicated, then refold in two.

2. Fold and unfold the sides to the center.

Lower Section

3. Fold the points to the outside, dividing the bottom angles in two, then turn over.

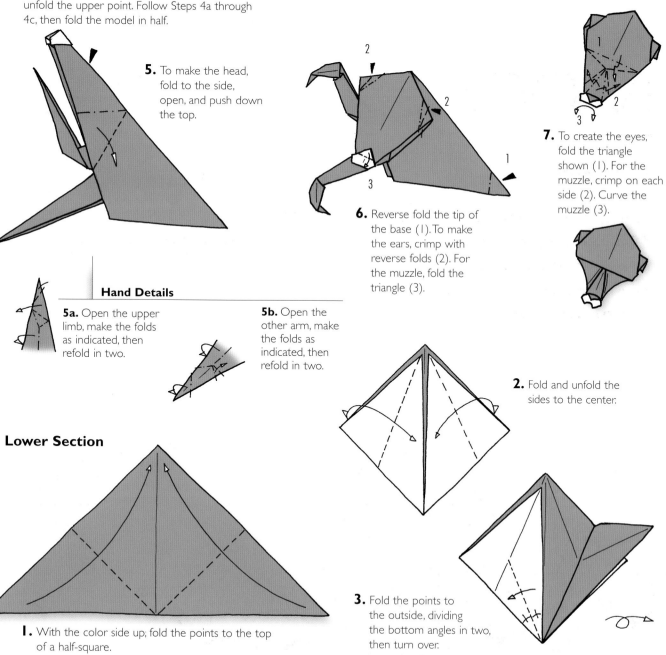

1. With the color side up, fold the points to the top of a half-square.

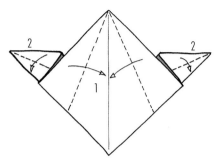

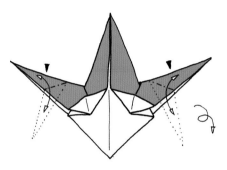

4. Note the folds and begin to fold the sides to the center (1) and the points in half (2).

5. To make the triangle flat as on the right, spread the raised section, slide a finger between the layers, and gently flatten as shown on the right side.

6. To make the legs, make reverse folds, then turn over.

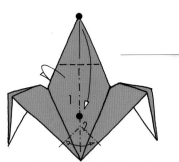

Tab Assembly Details

7a. Fold up the point.

7b. Crease as on the right.

7c. Make the creases reverse folds as on the right.

7. Fold the upper triangle (1) and crease the lower square. Follow Steps 7a through 7c before folding the model in two along the vertical axis.

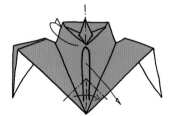

9. Bring out the tail, then fold the lower square, fitting the left side between the layers on the right. The model will refold automatically in two with some volume.

10. For the feet, make inside reverse folds (see p. 5).

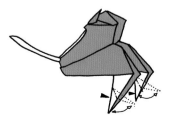

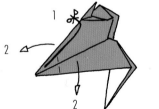

8. Cut the tail (1), then open the model (2).

Assembly Details

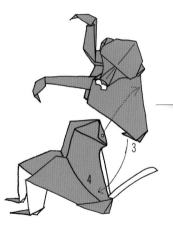

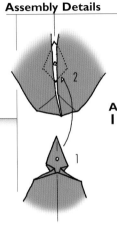

Assembly

11. Slide the tab of the lower section (1) between the central layers of the upper section (2). Slide the reverse fold at the base of the upper section (3) in the notch of the lower section (4).